BRUMBACK LIBRARY

3 3045 00176 1200

W9-ALM-031

$14.99

j242.82 Elkins, Stephen
ELK   The Jabez prayer
          collection : 30
          life-changing prayers

CHILDREN'S DEPARTMENT
THE BRUMBACK LIBRARY
OF VAN WERT COUNTY
VAN WERT, OHIO

The Jabez Prayer
COLLECTION
30 Life-Changing Prayers from the Bible for Children

- *The Lord's Prayer*
- *Hannah's Prayer*
- *Samuel's Prayer*
- *David's Prayer*

AND MANY MORE!

Written by Stephen Elkins • Narrated by Rebecca St. James
Illustrated by Ellie Colton

BROADMAN
& HOLMAN
PUBLISHERS

Nashville, Tennessee

J242.82
ELK

*This book is lovingly dedicated to my father,
Charles K. Elkins, whose love and Christian outreach
have touched the hearts and lives of the hurting,
and brought hope and joy to family and friends.
Yes, the world needs more fathers like you!*

———————

Copyright © 2001 by Stephen Elkins
Published in 2001 by Broadman & Holman Publishers
Nashville, Tennessee

Benediction Blessing, Come and See, and *Jabez,* Copyright ©2001.
Words and music by Stephen Elkins (Kenna Music, BMI). International
copyright secured. All rights reserved.

All Scripture quotations unless otherwise noted are from the
HOLY BIBLE, NEW INTERNATIONAL VERSION®,
copyright © 1973, 1978, 1984 by International Bible Society. Used by
permission of Zondervan Publishing House. All rights reserved.

Cover design and layout by Ed Maksimowicz

A catalog record for this book is available
from the Library of Congress.

All rights reserved. Printed in Belgium.

ISBN 0-8054-2579-9

1 2 3 4 5   05 04 03 02 01

14.99

Table of Contents

THE PRAYER OF ABRAM

Abram and Sarai had waited a very long time for a child. They began to think God had forgotten them. One night, Abram knelt and prayed:

O Sovereign Lord, what can you give me since I remain childless… You have given me no children; so a servant in my household will be my heir.
(Genesis 15:2-3)

God answered Abram's prayer saying, "You will have a son! Look up at the sky and count the stars. That's how many descendants you will have." Abram trusted God, and soon Isaac was born.

My prayer for today: *Dear Lord, help me to trust in You.*

THE PRAYER OF JACOB

Jacob and Esau were the twin sons of Isaac and Rebekah. Esau, the oldest son, was entitled to all the blessings of the first-born. But Jacob tricked their father into giving the blessing to him. Esau was very angry and said he would kill Jacob for doing this. Jacob earnestly prayed:

Deliver me, I pray. (Genesis 32:10, KJV)

When the two brothers finally met again, the Lord helped Esau to forgive Jacob. The brothers were once again friends.

My prayer for today: *Dear Lord, teach me to forgive others.*

THE PRAYER OF DEBORAH

Deborah loved the Lord and did what was pleasing in God's sight. For a short time, Deborah was the leader of Israel and many people sought her advice. When a mighty army threatened the people, God spoke to Deborah advising the army to fight. Deborah was present to see Israel defeat their enemy.

She gave thanks to God saying:

I will sing to the Lord, I will sing; I will make music to the Lord, the God of Israel. (Judges 5:3)

God used Deborah to show His power. Because she listened to God there were 40 years of peace in the land.

My prayer for today: *Dear Lord, help me to devote my life to following You.*

THE PRAYER OF SAMSON

Manoah and his wife had no children. Then an angel brought them news that they would have a very special baby boy. Samson was born and grew to be very strong because God's spirit was upon him. But Samson disobeyed the Lord and his strength left him. In his final hour, Samson prayed:

O Sovereign Lord, remember me. O God, please strengthen me just once more. (Judges 16:28)

The Lord heard Samson's prayer and restored his strength one last time.

My prayer for today: *Dear Lord, give me strength to do Your will.*

THE PRAYER OF HANNAH

Hannah was heartbroken because she had no children. She knelt before the Lord and asked Him to bless her with a child. The Lord granted her request and gave her a beautiful baby boy named Samuel. Hannah thanked God by praying:

My heart rejoices in the Lord... There is no one holy like the Lord; there is no one besides you; there is no Rock like our God. (1 Samuel 2:1,2)

Hannah joyfully dedicated Samuel to the Lord. Samuel grew to become a great servant of the Lord.

My prayer for today: *Dear Lord, thank You for answered prayer.*

THE PRAYER OF SOLOMON

Solomon, the son of David, became king after his father died. Solomon was the wisest man in all the world. He honored God by building a temple where the people could come and worship. On the day the temple was dedicated, Solomon stood before the people and prayed:

O Lord, God of Israel, there is no God like you in heaven above or on earth below—you who keep your covenant of love with your servants who continue wholeheartedly in your way. (1 Kings 8:23)

Solomon blessed the Lord and gave thanks for all the good things God had done.

My prayer for today: *Dear Lord, thank You for all the good things You have done for me.*

THE PRAYER OF JABEZ

Jabez was a very honorable man who loved the Lord. His mother named him Jabez which means painful, because his birth had been very painful. When Jabez became a man, he prayed to become a great servant of God with a far-reaching ministry. Jabez prayed:

Oh, that you would bless me and enlarge my territory!
Let your hand be with me, and keep me from harm
so that I will be free from pain. (1 Chronicles 4:10)

And God granted Jabez all that he requested.

My prayer for today: *Dear Lord, bless my service to You.*

THE PRAYER OF ASA

Asa was one of the good kings of Judah. He knew the secret of a successful life was doing the things God asked him to do. Asa trusted God and relied on His word. One day when Asa was to go into battle he prayed:

Lord, there is no one like you to help the powerless against the mighty. Help us, O Lord our God, for we rely on you… O Lord, you are our God.
(2 Chronicles 14:11)

Asa relied on God's power during times of trouble. God answered his prayer and Asa's army won the battle.

My prayer for today: *Dear Lord, help me to trust and obey You, even in times of trouble.*

THE PRAYER OF JEHOSHAPHAT

A great multitude of enemy soldiers had come against Israel to do battle. Jehoshaphat, Israel's leader, was afraid his nation would be destroyed. So he called upon all the people to fast and pray to God. All the people heard Jehoshaphat pray:

O our God… we have no might against this great company that cometh against us; neither know we what to do; but our eyes are upon thee.
(2 Chronicles 20:12, KJV)

God answered Jehoshaphat's prayer through the prophet Jahaziel who told the people not to be afraid or discouraged because God was in control. The battle was not theirs, but the Lord's. Keep your eyes fixed on the Lord and He will be with you.

My prayer for today: *Dear Lord, may I always keep my eyes fixed upon You.*

THE PRAYER OF NEHEMIAH

Nehemiah worked in the palace of the king of Persia. When he learned the walls of Jerusalem had been broken down and the gates burned, Nehemiah sat down and wept. He wanted to go back to Jerusalem and help rebuild the walls. But he could not do so without the king's blessing. So Nehemiah prayed:

O Lord, let your ear be attentive to the prayer of this your servant and to the prayer of your servants who delight in revering your name...(and grant me) favor in the presence of (the king). (Nehemiah 1:11)

When Nehemiah asked the king to allow him to go to Jerusalem, "Yes," said the king. "Go and help rebuild the wall!"

My prayer for today: *Dear Lord, give me a job to do just for You.*

THE PRAYER OF DAVID

David praised the Lord for His marvelous creation and power. He humbled himself before the Lord and asked for grace and forgiveness. In his sincere desire to please God, David prayed:

Let the words of my mouth, and the meditation of my heart, be acceptable in thy sight, O Lord, my strength, and my redeemer. (Psalm 19:14, KJV)

David wanted to please the Lord in everything he did.

My prayer for today: *Dear Lord, may what I say be pleasing to You.*

THE PRAYER OF DAVID

David had confidence in prayer. He believed that God would hear his request and answer him. On this day, David asked the Lord to protect him from his enemies and to teach him to be a better child of God. David prayed:

Unto thee, O Lord, do I lift up my soul. O my God, I trust in thee: let me not be ashamed, let not mine enemies triumph over me. (Psalm 25:1-2, KJV)

David was certainly a man after God's own heart. In times of trouble he always turned to the Lord.

My prayer for today: *Dear Lord, teach me to pray.*

THE PRAYER OF DAVID

When David sinned, he prayed earnestly for forgiveness. He asked the Lord to change his heart so that he would not sin again. David prayed for God to again give him the joy that comes from knowing Him.

Create in me a pure heart, O God, and renew a steadfast spirit within me. Restore to me the joy of your salvation and grant me a willing spirit, to sustain me. (Psalm 51:10,12)

No matter what we have done, God will always love us. His grace and love are bigger than any sin.

My prayer for today: *Dear Lord, forgive me when I sin.*

THE PRAYER OF ETHAN

Ethan did not understand why God was taking so long to fulfill His promise. God had promised that someone from David's family would always be king. God also promised He would always protect them. Ethan prayed:

I will sing of the mercies of the Lord for ever. With my mouth will I make known thy faithfulness to all generations. (Psalm 89:1, KJV)

Ethan knew God was faithful and that one day an heir of David, Christ the Lord, would reign forever!

My prayer for today: *Dear Lord, give me patience to wait for Your perfect timing.*

31

THE PRAYER OF MOSES

Moses knew that without the help of the Lord, he could do nothing. The Lord had shown Moses His power many times. Moses had seen God's power in the burning bush and in the parting of the Red Sea. Moses knew the power of prayer. Moses loved God and served Him. Moses prayed:

Lord, thou hast been our dwelling place in all generations… let the beauty of the Lord our God be upon us: and establish thou the work of our hands.
(Psalm 90:1,17, KJV)

Moses prayed that the people of Israel would grow in wisdom and be successful in everything they did.

My prayer for today: *Dear Lord, may I grow in the wisdom of Your Word.*

THE PRAYER OF DAVID

David asked God to help him understand the written instructions He had left us in the Bible. David recognized that without the guidance we get from God's Word we are destined to lose our way.

Thy word is a lamp unto my feet, and a light unto my path. (Psalm 119:105, KJV)

We each need a lamp to show us the way through the dark. God's Word is the lamp that never goes out.

My prayer for today: *Dear Lord, may Your Word always brighten my path.*

THE PRAYER OF JEREMIAH

God spoke to Jeremiah and commanded him to purchase a field from his cousin. God told Jeremiah this would be a sign that He would one day restore His people and return them to Jerusalem. After Jeremiah did all that God had instructed, he prayed:

Ah, Sovereign Lord, you have made the heavens and the earth by your great power and out-stretched arm. Nothing is too hard for you. (Jeremiah 32:17)

God's people had disobeyed Him for years and were scattered throughout the land. But Jeremiah knew that nothing was impossible for God.

My prayer for today: *Dear Lord, help me to listen for Your instructions.*

THE PRAYER OF DANIEL

Throughout his life Daniel had a strong faith in God. He prayed to God every day. He encouraged God's people to remain faithful to God's commandments. When God's people disobeyed, Daniel prayed:

"O Lord, the great and awesome God, who keeps his covenant of love with all who love him and obey his commands, we have sinned and done wrong. The Lord our God is merciful and forgiving, even though we have rebelled against him." (Daniel 9:4,5,9)

In his prayer Daniel says that God will always love us regardless of what we do.

My prayer for today: *Dear Lord, help me to be faithful throughout my life.*

THE PRAYER OF JONAH

Jonah disobeyed God by sailing to Tarshish instead of going to Nineveh. At sea a great storm suddenly came up. Knowing his disobedience had caused the storm, Jonah confessed to the others and was thrown overboard. God rescued Jonah by allowing him to be swallowed by a big fish. Jonah prayed:

In my distress I called to the Lord, and he answered me. When my life was ebbing away, I remembered you, Lord, and my prayer rose to you, to your holy temple… Salvation comes from the Lord. (Jonah 2:1,7,9)

Jonah suffered the consequences of disobedience, but prayed for forgiveness. God granted him a second chance. This time Jonah obeyed.

My prayer for today: *Dear Lord, thank You for hearing my prayers and forgiving my sins.*

THE PRAYER OF MICAH

Micah warned the people that their disobedience would result in God's judgement. He spoke of a time when people would no longer be able to trust their neighbors, friends, or family. But God, our heavenly Father, pardons and forgives us when we disobey. Micah prayed:

I watch in hope for the Lord, I wait for God my Savior; my God will hear me. (Micah 7:7)

Micah told the people God would bless them if they would ask for forgiveness.

My prayer for today: *Dear Lord, thank You for being my closest friend.*

THE PRAYER OF HABAKKUK

The prophet Habakkuk knew the real secret of lasting happiness was not found in the things of earth. Habakkuk said he would rejoice even if the fig tree did not bloom. He would be happy even if there were no grapes on the vine, no sheep in the pasture, or cattle in the stalls. He prayed:

Yet I will rejoice in the Lord, I will be joyful in God my Savior. The Sovereign Lord is my strength. (Habakkuk 3:18-19)

We, too, should rejoice because God is in control.

My prayer for today: *Dear Lord, I am happy because You love me.*

THE LORD'S PRAYER

In the Sermon on the Mount Jesus gave instructions for living. He also gave His followers an example of how to pray:

Our Father which art in heaven, Hallowed be thy name. Thy kingdom come. Thy will be done in earth as it is in heaven. Give us this day our daily bread. And forgive us our debts, as we forgive our debtors. And lead us not into temptation, but deliver us from evil: For thine is the kingdom, and the power, and the glory, for ever. Amen
(Matthew 6:9-13, KJV)

This is how we should pray!

My prayer for today: *Dear Lord, help me learn to pray as You taught us.*

THE PRAYER OF MARY

God chose a very special girl named Mary to be the mother of Jesus. Mary loved the Lord and had a heart that was pure and true. When the angel told Mary that she was to be the mother of the Messiah, Mary lifted up her heart in praise and thanksgiving:

My soul glorifies the Lord and my spirit rejoices in God my Savior, for he has been mindful of the humble state of his servant. (Luke 1:46-47)

God blessed Mary and had a very special plan for her.

My prayer for today: *Dear Lord, lead me as I discover what Your plan is for my life.*

THE PRAYER OF JESUS

Jesus sent His disciples out two by two. He instructed them to go ahead and prepare the people for His coming. When His followers returned they were happy because Jesus had given them the ability to heal people. Jesus reminded them not to rejoice because He had given them this power, but to rejoice because they believed in the Father.

I praise you, Father, Lord of heaven and earth, because you have hidden these things from the wise and learned, and revealed them to little children. (Luke 10:21)

Pure and simple faith, like a child, is what Jesus expects from us.

My prayer for today: *Dear Lord, I trust You.*

THE PRAYER OF JESUS

Jesus knew that His time on earth was nearly over, so He prayed for His followers. He asked His heavenly Father to bless and protect them as they continued the ministry He had started. Jesus prayed:

"My prayer is not for them alone. I pray also for those who will believe in me through their message, that all of them may be one, Father, just as you are in me and I am in you. May they also be in us so that the world may believe that you have sent me." (John 17:20-21)

Jesus prayed that His followers would be unified in one spirit so the world would know that He was God's Son.

My prayer for today: *Dear Lord, thank You that You loved us enough to die so that we might have eternal life.*

THE APOSTLES' PRAYER

After the apostle Judas betrayed Jesus, the eleven remaining apostles agreed that they must choose another apostle in order to fulfill Scripture. Led by Peter, the apostles narrowed their choices to two men. Then they prayed and asked God to show them which of the two should take Judas' place.

"Lord, you know everyone's heart. Show us which of these two you have chosen to take over this... ministry." (Acts 1:24-25)

God helped them see that Matthias was the best choice.

My prayer for today: *Dear Lord, guide me as I make decisions today.*

THE PRAYER OF PAUL

The apostle Paul asked his friends to pray for him on many occasions. He knew that God would hear the prayers of his friends and supply every need. Paul prayed for them, too:

May the God of peace ... equip you with everything good for doing his will. (Hebrews 13:20)

Paul goes on to pray that the Lord will work through us to do those things which are pleasing in His sight.

My prayer for today: *Dear Lord, may all I do be pleasing to You.*

THE PRAYER OF PAUL

Spiritual leaders must not only pray for their followers, but they must also teach them the way to live. Paul prayed that believers might know and recognize the strength of the Holy Spirit in their lives.

I pray that out of his glorious riches he may strengthen you with power through his Spirit in your inner being, so that Christ may dwell in your hearts through faith. (Ephesians 3:16-17)

Paul continually prayed for others. He wanted them to see how important their role was in proclaiming the message of Christ.

My prayer for today: *Dear Lord, thank You for my family.*

THE PRAYER OF THE 24 ELDERS

Heaven is a wonderful place because God will be there. Those who believe in Jesus and have accepted Him as their Savior will be there too. There will be singing and great celebration forever and ever. Everyone will worship God and celebrate His wonderful love for us:

You are worthy, our Lord and God, to receive glory and honor and power, for you created all things, and by your will they were created and have their being. (Revelation 4:11)

God is the creator of all things and is worthy to be praised.

My prayer for today: *Dear Lord, thank You for Your great love.*

THE PRAYER OF HEAVEN

One day, all believers will stand before the throne of God in heaven. They will sing praises to the One who sent His only begotten Son. Their prayer will echo through the streets of heaven:

"Hallelujah! For our Lord God Almighty reigns. Let us rejoice and be glad and give him glory!"
(Revelation 19:6-7)

What a glorious day that will be, for on that day we will see Jesus!

My prayer for today: *Dear Lord, thank You for the promise of heaven.*

Books Also Available by Stephen Elkins

WORD & SONG BIBLE
0-8054-1689-7

Word & Song Bible with Cassettes
0-8054-1691-9

Word & Song Bible with CDs
0-8054-1690-0

Word & Song Bible CD 5-pack
0-8054-1692-7

Word & Song Bible Cassette 5-pack
0-8054-1693-5

Word & Song Bible Songbook #1 (OT) with Cassette
0-8054-1694-3

Word & Song Bible Songbook #2 (NT) with Cassette
0-8054-1695-1

Look for the Companion Album from Pamplin Records

The Jabez Prayer Song Collection
Sung by The Wonder Kids Choir
Produced by Stephen Elkins
CD Order # PRCD 2322
Cassette Order # PRCS 2322

WORD & SONG GREATEST BIBLE STORIES EVER TOLD SERIES *(Available Soon)*

God's Power with CD
0-8054-2466-0

Special Families with CD
0-8054-2467-9

Courage & Strength with CD
0-8054-2468-7

Stories that Build Character with CD
0-8054-2469-5

Stories of Faith with CD
0-8054-2470-9

LULLABIBLE
0-8054-2388-5

LullaBible with Cassettes
0-8054-2389-3

LullaBible with CDs
0-8054-2390-7

LullaBible Cassette 2-pack
0-8054-2391-5

LullaBible CD 2-pack
0-8054-2392-3

Available at Christian Bookstores Everywhere.